KNOCK~KNOCK KNEES AND FUNNY BONES

Riddles for Every Body

Judith Mathews *and* Fay Robinson

pictures by
Jack Desrocher

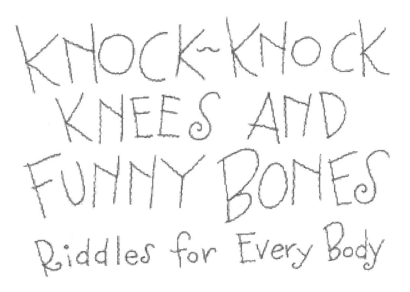

Albert Whitman & Company
Morton Grove, Illinois

To my big, tough aunt, Minnie Rivkin. J.M.

For my humorous friends. F.R.

To Addy and Hannah. J.D.

Library of Congress Cataloging-in-Publication Data

Mathews, Judith.
    Knock-knock knees and funny bones : riddles for every body/
Judith Mathews and Fay Robinson; illustrated by Jack Desrocher.
        p.   cm.
        ISBN 0-8075-4203-2
        1. Riddles, Juvenile.   2. Knock-knock jokes. [1. Riddles.
2. Knock-knock jokes. 3. Jokes.]   I. Robinson, Fay. II. Desrocher, Jack, ill.
III. Title.
PN6371. 5.M383   1994
398.6—dc20   93 -17899
                                                                   CIP
                                                                    AC

Design by Lucy Smith

Knock-knock.
Who's there?
Eye and Ear.
Eye and Ear who?
Eye got some jokes and riddles, and Ear they are!

The Inside Story

What do kidneys say at the start of every baseball game?
"Bladder up!"

If grownups have knees, what do children have?
Kidneys.

If grownups have colons, what do children have?
Semi-colons.

What monster has the biggest stomach?
The Abdominal Snowman.

How long can you hold your breath?
A lung, lung time.

What part of your body never dies?
Your liver.

Who plays the music when your insides have a birthday?
Your organs play spinal chords while your heart keeps the beat.

Why is the human body so easy to understand?
It's organ-ized.

Every Body Does It

Why isn't your nose twelve inches long?
If it were, it would be a foot!

What's the sharpest part of your body?
Your shoulder blades.

What did the leg say to the hip?
"Let's leave this joint!"

If you breathe oxygen during the day, what do you breathe at night?
Nitrogen.

If an athlete gets athlete's foot, what does an astronaut get?
Missile toe.

What relatives protect you from disease?
Your auntie-bodies.

On what island should you never go barefoot?
Krak-a-toe-a.

Where should you keep your old Valentine hearts?
In a chest, of course!

When can you see through a friend?
When she has a pane in her side.

Why should you never jog on an empty stomach?
It's easier to jog on your feet.

What can you hold without touching?
Your breath.

When did Benjamin Franklin discover electricity?
During a brainstorm.

Knock-knock.
Who's there?
Pitcher.
Pitcher who?
Pitcher right foot in, pitcher right foot out, pitcher right foot in, and you shake it all about!

Joe: *I'm a member of the belly club.*
Schmoe: *Oh, yeah?*
Joe: *Yeah—want to see my button?*

Why do knock knees come in pairs?
So they can tell each other knock-knock jokes.

Heads Up!

What can you do when you're late for the barber's?
Take the short cut.

How many ears does Davy Crockett have?
Three: his right ear, his left ear, and his wild front ear.

Why is your nose in the middle of your face?
Because it's the scenter.

Which hand should you use to brush your teeth?
Either one, but it's better to use a toothbrush.

Which football player wears the largest helmet?
The one with the largest head.

What kind of teeth can you get for a dollar?
Buck teeth.

Knock-knock.
Who's there?
Danielle.
Danielle who?
Danielle so loud—my ears are just fine!

What did the bald man say when he got a comb for his birthday?
"Thank you very much. I'll never part with it."

When are your eyes not your eyes?
When an onion makes them water.

When do tears appear?
During a cry-sis.

What did the right eye say to the left eye?
"Just between us, something smells!"

What is in front of your face that you only see in winter?
Your breath.

What part of your face likes libraries?
Eyebrows (I browse).

How can you tell if a computer has teeth?
If it bytes you.

What happens when your tongue gets tired?
It overslurps.

Boodles

Guess what these boodles are:

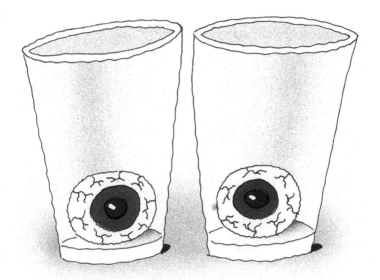

Eyeglasses

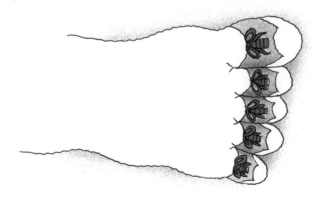

Toe shoes

Wishbone

Head stand

Tail tail!

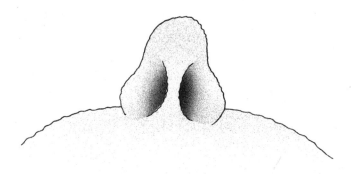

Your nose as seen by a spoon

Footstool

Knuckle head

Animal Crack-ups

What did the shark leave for the waitress?
A fingertip.

Why don't octopi ever join the Marines?
They'd rather be in the Arm-y.

What do turtles wear when it's cold outside?
People-neck sweaters.

What furry animal has amphibians on its feet?
The three-toad sloth.

Why couldn't the frog croak?
He had a man in his throat.

Why won't worms skydive?
They are spineless.

What do man-eating tigers drink with their burgers?
Handshakes.

What do animals do when they lose their tails?
They go to a re-tail store.

Why are daddy rabbits like balding men?
They both have a little hare.

Knock-knock.
Who's there?
Bull.
Bull who?
Bull in your stomach—you're slouching!

Why was the centipede so confused?
Because his mother told him to put his best foot forward.

Why did the shark ask the diver for help?
He needed a hand.

Why is a baby in a bathtub like an animal?
Because it's bare.

What do the boy squid and the girl squid do in the moonlight?
They stroll arm in arm in arm...

Why did the elephant eat a mothball every day?
To keep moths out of its trunk.

Laugh Your Leaves Off

What flowers are the best kissers?
Two-lips.

If you were a piece of fruit, where would you keep your seeds?
In your armpits.

What did the endive say at the finish line?
"I'm a-head of lettuce!"

Why do cornfields like Halloween?
Because it's ear-ie.

What does celery use for stockings?
Garden hose.

Why do roses have such strong legs?
From petal-ing.

Why does corn have such strong legs?
From stalk-ing.

What type of tree is filled with bodies?
A family tree.

A Handful of Puzzlers

What has a back, four legs, and two arms—but no head?
A chair.

What has no feet but always wears out shoes?
A sidewalk.

What has one foot on each end and a foot in the middle?
A yardstick.

What has a head and a mouth, but no eyes, nose, or ears?
A river.

What has many teeth, but cannot chew?
A saw.

What has a neck but no head?
A bottle.

What has a tongue but cannot speak?
A gym shoe.

What can push people around, fly, and whistle, but has no body at all?
The wind.

Kneed Any More?

Why do children laugh at their elbows?
Because that's where their funny bones are.

What question can't you answer "yes" to?
"Are you sleeping?"

Why did the boy put his legs in the cow pen at the county fair?
He wanted to enter his calves in the contest.

What part of you disappears when you stand up?
Your lap.

Why are authors so funny looking?
Because tales come from their heads.

Why did Ben refuse to go ice skating?
He had cold feet.

What happened when Maria tripped on the sprinkler?
She got a sprayed ankle.

Why did Alyson pour car wax into the toolbox?
She wanted to polish her nails.

Why did the baby have white hair?
Because his near-sighted mother kept powdering the wrong end.

What's the hardest kind of bow to tie?
An elbow.

What do you get when you cross a fish with a tiger?
An animal with fin-GRRS.

In what school activity do your guts do best?
In-testin'.

What catches flies and has eighteen legs?
A baseball team.

What's the difference between a bald man and a mother gorilla?
One has no hair apparent and the other is a hairy parent.

What did the pelvis say when it won the hula contest?
"Hip, hip, hooray!"

When do you lose your sense of touch?
When you don't feel well.

How can you tell if the school custodian is in love with your teacher?
If he sweeps her off her feet.

Knock-knock.
Who's there?
Razor.
Razor who?
Razor hand if you have a question.

Why do blood cells never get lost?
They know the way by heart.

Whose snack is stuck in your throat?
Adam's apple.

What magazine do smart stomachs prefer?
Reader's Digest-ion.

Knock-knock.
Who's there?
Frank's eye.
Frank's eye who?
Frank's, eye needed some laughs!

About the Authors and Illustrator

Between them, **Fay Robinson** and **Judith Mathews** have four knees (not knock), some very funny bones, and more tales than they can count. Each is the author of several books for children, and together they have written *Oh, How Waffle! Riddles You Can Eat* and *Nathaniel Willy, Scared Silly*.

Tired of crowds and commuting in the San Francisco Bay Area, **Jack Desrocher** and his family moved in 1989 to an Ozark farm they affectionately call Flying Goat Ranch. Their haven has since grown crowded with horses, goats, chickens, ducks, bunnies, kittens, and a dog. Jack now dodges animals en route to his backyard studio rather than semis on the Bay Bridge.